UMAMI world recipe Vol. 1

JAPANESE

Contents

UMAMI – a new word for an old taste

It was not until very recently that Umami was recognized as a basic taste. For the most part, vague, even contradictory descriptions have had to suffice.

In Japan, however, researchers had a head start in formulating the concept and clearing up the confusion. With their traditional diet of simple, uncooked food, the Japanese have been particularly attuned to the subtleties of flavour. Given this heritage, it was only natural that words necessary to describe this culinary experience would evolve, and it was only natural that the nation's scientists would explore the roots of a description such as Umami, which was merely a term of approbation for centuries.

A key step in understanding the chemical source of Umami came around the turn of last century when it was isolated from "dashi", although its function remained unrecognized for decades to come. Taking a break from his research at Tokyo Imperial University, Professor Kikunae Ikeda settled down to a bowl of tofu in a broth made with kelp. That traditional Japanese dish turned out to be momentous for Ikeda was struck by the way that the broth made the tofu particularly delicious.

Bringing the work of others to bear, he went on to explore the origins of this taste and isolated glutamic acid as its basis. He named it Umami, and the word moved from dining tables to scientific conference tables. The reason Umami had gone unrecognized for so long, he noted, was partially because this delicate taste tended to blend in so well with others.

Ikeda's progeny followed up his findings with the identification of Umami substances. Even if all the results are not in yet the evidence is telling. Reinforcement of the suggestion that Umami is a basic taste comes partly from repeated failures to synthesize this taste from compounds of the traditional four (sweet, sour, salty and bitter). Half a century after the watershed wrought by Ikeda's insights, still more evidence has emerged to establish Umami as fundamental. Generally, a basic taste is induced through specific receptors that react only to certain stimuli. Recent findings by Dr. Kenzo Kurihara of Hokkaido University and Dr. Yojiro Kawamura of Osaka University indicate that monosodium glutamate representing Umami substances has its own receptor sites in the alfactory cells of aquatic animals and taste cells.

By 1979, Japanese scientists had introduced their results to the rest of the world in a paper on "The Umami Taste" at the joint U.S.-Japan Science Conference. The conclusion was inescapable. For too long, researchers had focused only on four tastes, and, consequently, described only four — even though they had recognized that the matrix outlined by the German psychologist Hans Henning in 1916 was insufficient. Finally, here was an explanation that accounted for some of the question marks in taste physiology.

In both laboratories and kitchens, the concept and word, Umami are gaining ground. Not only have they won scientific standing, but gradually more and more people are acknowledging umami as a key to gastronomical delights.

TRADITIONAL SIMMERED CHICKEN AND VEGETABLES

Serves 4

150g chicken thighs	100g bamboo shoot (boiled)	⌐ <A>
3-5 dried shiitake mushrooms	20g mange tout (boiled and cut in half)	2 tbsp sugar
1 small carrot	150g konnyaku	2 tbsp sake
100g lotus root	200ml Japanese soup stock (see page 28)	2 tbsp soy sauce (light coloured, if available)
100g burdock root	1 tbsp vegetable oil	a pinch of Umami seasoning └

1   Cut the chicken into bite size pieces. Soak the mushrooms in 100ml water for 10 minutes, remove the stems and cut in half. Keep the shiitake water.

2   Cut all the vegetables (ex. mange tout) into bite size pieces. Soak the burdock root in water and the lotus root in vinegared water for a while. Boil the konnyaku lightly.

3   Heat the oil in a pan and stir-fry the chicken. Then cut the vegetables. Add the soup stock, shiitake water and bring to the boil.

4   Add <A> and simmer for 30 mintes. Add the mange tout just before removing from the heat.

SIMMERED MACKEREL IN GRATED DAIKON

Serves 4

4 pieces mackerel (150-200g each)

300g daikon (Japanese radish)

1/3 tsp salt

a pinch of Umami seasoning

2 chives (chopped)

3 tbsp mirin

some plain flour

vegetable oil for deep-flying

<A>
- 1/3 tsp salt
- a pinch of Umami seasoning

<B>
- 150ml Japanese soup stock (see page 28)
- 3 tbsp soy sauce
- a pinch of Umami seasoning

1 Rub <A> onto the mackerel and leave for 10 minutes. Grate the daikon and drain lightly.

2 Coat the mackerel with the flour thinly and deep-fry until browned.

3 Place the mirin in a pan and bring to the boil. Add <B> and bring to the boil again. Then add the mackerel and simmer for a few minutes. Sprinkle the daikon on top and remove from the heat.

4 Serve with the broth. Garnish with the chives.

SIMMERED CHUNKY POTATO WITH SLICED BEEF

Serves 4

200g beef, thin sliced

500g potato

1 onion

1 fragment ginger (sliced)

1 tbsp garden peas (boiled)

300ml Japanese soup stock (see page 28)

1 tbsp vegetable oil

<A>

2 tbsp sugar

2 tbsp sake

2 tbsp soy sauce

a pinch of Umami seasoning

1   Cut the beef into bite size pieces. Peel the potato, cut into bite size pieces and soak in water. Cut the onion into wedge-shaped pieces.

2   Heat the oil in a pan and stir-fry the ginger. Add the beef and drained potato. Add the onion and soup stock, bring to the boil and skim off any scum that forms during cooking.

3   Add <A> and simmer until the ingredients have become soft. Mix the garden peas just before removing from the heat.

GRILLED SALMON WITH GARLIC AND GINGER PICKLES

Serves 4

4 pieces salmon (120-150g each)

1 tsp salt

1/2 tsp Umami seasoning

40g ginger

1/2 tsp ground garlic (or garlic powder)

4 wedged slices of lemon or lime

<A>

200ml water

50ml rice vinegar

a pinch of salt

a pinch of Umami seasoning

1 Rub the salt and Umami seasoning into the salmon and leave overnight.

2 Slice the ginger, cut each slice into a leaf shape, make fine slits and pickle in <A>.overnight.

3 Rub the garlic powder into the salmon and grill, or stir-fry both sides.

4 Serve with lemon and sliced ginger.

STIR-FRIED AUBERGINE WITH SPICY SAUCE

Serves 4

6 Japanese aubergine
(or 2 Western aubergine)

2 tbsp vegetable oil

40ml hot water

<A>

1 tsp chopped ginger

1 tsp chopped garlic

2 tbsp chopped spring onion

1 tbsp ground sesame seeds

4 tbsp soy sauce

1/2 chili oil

a pinch of Umami seasoning

---

1   Cut the calyx out of the aubergines. Heat the oil in a frying pan and stir-fry the aubergines until the colour of the skin has turned brown.

2   Add the hot water, add a lid, and cook for another 5 minutes (Takes twice the time for Western aubergine). Tear the aubergine into bite size strips.

3   Mix the ingredients of <A> well and pour onto the aubergine when serving.

VEGETABLE AND SEAFOOD TEMPURA

Serves 4

4 prawns

4 shiitake mushrooms

200g aubergine

100g green pepper

100g sweet potato

<Dipping Sauce>

200ml Japanese soup stock (see page 28)

50ml soy sauce

50ml mirin

a pinch of Umami seasoning

80-100g grated daikon (Japanese radish)(optional)

<Batter Coating>

150ml cold water

100g plain flour

1 egg

1/2 tsp Umami seasoning

<tip: you may use any seafood/vegetables you like – e.g. squid, cod, carrot, squash etc, but watery vegetables should be avoided.>

How to make tempura dipping sauce · · · · · · · · · · · · · ·

You may enjoy tempura with salt or soy sauce but it is worth trying with this traditional dipping sauce.

1 Place the Japanese soup stock, mirin, soy sauce and Umami seasoning in a sauce pan, bring to the boil and leave to cool. Optionally, serve with some grated daikon.

How to make the batter coating · · · · · · · · · · · · · · · · · ·

The secret of nice crispy tempura is to mix the batter properly, using chopsticks.

1 Break the egg into a bowl, add water (the colder, the better) and mix well.

2 Add the flour and Umami seasoning, sifting out any lumps then mix together with chopsticks, moving them to the right and left. Don't move them in a circular motion, or the tempura will not crisp when fried.

N.B.
Once made, use up immediately. Do not leave for more than 20 minutes.

How to cook tempura ·····························

1 Wash the prawns in salt water and remove the heads. Remove all the shell except for the tail and the part nearest to it. Make a couple of cuts on the underside.

2 Wash the shiitake mushrooms and cut off the stems. Curve a cross on the surface of each mushroom.

3 Slice the aubergine and sweet potato diagonally into thin slices. Cut the green pepper in quarters, lengthways (if using Japanese petit green pepper, cut in half.)

4 Cover the ingredients with oil and heat to 180 degrees in a deep frying pan. (You can test that the oil is hot enough by dropping a small amount of batter mixture in the pan. It should form a crisp batter immediately.)

5 Dip the ingredients in the batter and fry immediately. When they begin to change colour, remove them from the pan and place on kitchen paper to drain any excess oil.

How to fry tempura perfectly

Cook the vegetables first, then the seafood afterwards. The hard vegetables (i.e. sweet potato, squash) should be cooked carefully, making sure the oil is at the right temperature. To cook watery seafood (i.e. fish, squid), cover thinly with flour before dipping in batter, to prevent the oil from splashing up when frying.

VEGETABLE SUSHI SCATTERED STYLE

Serves 4

450g short grain rice

630ml water

10cm x 5cm dried kombu (optional)

80g burdock root

80g carrot

120g bamboo shoot (boiled)

80g lotus root

50g mange tout

some rice vinegar and salt

\<A\>

100ml rice vinegar

2&1/2 tbsp sugar

1 tsp salt

a pinch of Umami seasoning

\<B\>

200ml Japaese soup stock (see page 28)

1 tbsp mirin

1 tbsp sugar

1&1/3 tbsp soy sauce

a pinch of Umami seasoning

\<C\>

100ml Japanese soup stock

1 tbsp mirin

1 tbsp soy sauce

\<D\>

2 tbsp rice vinegar

1 tbsp Japanese soup stock

1 tbsp sugar

a pinch of salt

a pinch of Umami seasoning

\<Tip: In addition to the ingredients, it is common to use thin strips of nori seaweed, and pickled ginger as toppings.\>

How to make Sushi Rice ·························

To cook sushi rice, it is important to remember that the rice should be cooked with less water than usual, and vinegar added to it while hot. Here is how to cook the perfect sushi rice.

1   Wash the rice and cook with 630ml water and kombu. When cooked, remove the kombu and place the rice in a flat-bottomed bowl. Mix <A> well, and pour over the rice.

2   Mix the rice swiftly with a flat spatula, but not mashing it, just allowing the vinegar contact with all of the rice. Use your strength evenly when handling the spatula, and when mixing the rice, move the spatula as if scooping the rice rather than blending it.

3   Cool the rice down swiftly using a paper fan, and gently turn the rice with the spatula. Fanning the rice prevents it from being overly sticky, and also adds lustre.

How to cook vegetable sushi ·

1   Wash the burdock root, peel, cut into fine strips, 3cm in length, and soak in vinegared water. Cut the carrot into the same size pieces as the burdock root.

2   Slice the bamboo shoot thinly into 2cm x 2cm pieces. Slice the lotus root thinly, and soak in vinegared water.

3   Trim the mange tout, boil lightly in salted water and cut diagonally into thin strips.

4   Drain the burdock root and simmer with <B> until the broth is reduced to nothing.

5   Boil the carrot in lightly salted and vinegared water. Simmer the bamboo shoot with <C>.

6   Boil the lotus root with lightly vinegared water and then soak in <D> for 10 minutes.

7   Drain all the vegetables and mix them (ex. mange tout) with the sushi rice. Top with mange tout when serving.

RICE WITH CHICKEN AND VEGETABLES

Serves 4

300g short grain rice

360ml water

150g chicken thigh

1/2 carrot

4 dried shiitake mushrooms

150g burdock root

4 chives (or spring onions)

<A>
- 1 tbsp sake
- 1 tbsp soy sauce
- 1 tsp ginger juice

<B>
- 2 tbsp sake
- 2 tbsp mirin
- 2 tbsp soy sauce
- a pinch of Umami seasoning

1 Wash the rice, drain and leave for 30 minutes. Cut the chicken into 8mm cubes and soak in <A> for 10 minutes.

2 Soak the mushrooms, remove the stems and cut into 6mm cubes. Cut the carrot and burdock root into 6mm pieces and soak the burdock root in vinegared water.

3 Place the rice in a rice cooker (or a deep pan with a lid) and mix <B>. then place the ingredients on top and cook. Mix well when cooked. Serve with chopped chives.

SAVORY STICKY RICE IN SQUID

Makes 6 pieces

6 squid

170g sticky rice
(glutinous rice)

1 tsp soy sauce

<A>

100ml sake

100ml soy sauce

2 tbsp sugar

a pinch of Umami seasoning

---

1   Wash the rice and soak overnight. Remove the legs, bones and organs from the squid and wash lightly.

2   Stuff the squid with rice, leaving enough space (30-40%) as rice swells when cooked. Put a short skewer in the end.

3   Place the squid in a pan, making sure they don't pile up. Pour on water to cover them, and add <A>.

4   Cover the squid with a piece of cooking foil slightly smaller than the pan in diameter and simmer for 1 hour. Slice before serving.

SOBA NOODLE SOUP WITH CHICKEN

Serves 4

400g soba noodles (cooked)

200g chicken thigh

1 spring onion

1500ml Japanese soup stock (see below)

60ml soy sauce

60ml mirin

a pinch of Umami seasoning

How to make Japanese soup stock · · · · · · · · · · · · · · · · ·

Japanese soup stock, aka dashi, is the most important element of the authentic Japanese taste. As you can see from this book, many Japanese traditional dishes include dashi. The recipe is much simpler than you think!

Makes 1500ml

10cm × 10cm dried kombu (kelp)

1500ml water

20g bonito flakes

Make a few slits in the kombu and cook it in the water on a medium heat. Remove the kelp just before it boils and add the bonito flakes. Bring to the boil and strain.

How to make vegetarian soup stock · · · · · · · · · · · · · · ·

For vegetarians, you may use twice as much kombu and omit the bonito from the recipe above, but here is another traditional recipe suitable for them.

Makes 1500ml

6-7 dried shiitake mushrooms

1500ml water

Simply place the mushrooms in the water, leave for at least 1 hour, then strain. If you do not have time, boil once and leave for 10 minutes. The mushrooms from the stock can be used as a cooking ingredient.

Other ingredients for soup stock

Another popular ingredient for dashi is iriko (often called niboshi) – This is especially suitable for miso soup. Various kinds of instant stock are also available in sachets, liquid and powdered form.

How to make Soba Noodles with Chicken · · · · · · · · · ·

1   Cut the chicken into bite size pieces.

2   Boil the mirin in a pan to remove the alcohol, add the soup stock and bring to
    the boil. Add the soy sauce and Umami seasoning and bring to the boil again.

3   Add the chicken and cook until tender, skimming off any scum that forms
    during cooking.

4   Place the cooked noodles in a deep bowl and pour the soup and chicken
    on top. Garnish with chopped spring onion.

Tips for cooking soba perfectly

Place the dried soba in boiling water, adding a cup of water if it bubbles
over. If it bubbles over again, lower the heat. The cooking time depends on
the thickness of the noodle (it is normally indicated on the package). Once
cooked; drain, rinse, squeeze and turn under cold running water.

FRIED UDON WITH PORK AND VEGETABLES

Serves 4

400g udon noodles (boiled)

200g lean pork

200g cabbage

2 carrots

2 leeks

2 tbsp vegetable oil

20g bonito flakes (optional)

\<A\>

2 tbsp soy sauce

4 tsp sake

some salt and pepper

a pinch of Umami seasoning

1   Drain the boiled noodles well. Cut the pork into 1cm cubes. Cut the cabbage into strips, 2cm in width, the carrots into fine strips, 2mm x 5cm, and slice the leeks diagonally, 5mm.

2   Heat the oil in a frying pan and fry the pork and vegetables. When cooked add the noodles.

3   Add A to season. Serve on a plate and garnish with bonito flakes.

MISO SOUP
WITH WAKAME AND TOFU

Serves 4

10g dried wakame seaweed

140g silken tofu
(1/3-1/2 size block)

40g white miso

600g Japanese soup stock
(see page 28)

a handful of chives

a pinch of Umami seasoning

---

1 Soak the wakame in water for 5 minutes, then cut into bite size pieces. Cut the tofu into 1.5cm cubes.

2 Heat the soup stock for 3-4 minutes and gently dissolve the miso in the soup.

3 Add the wakame and tofu and heat gently for 5 minutes being careful not to let it boil. Sprinkle on the Umami. Season just before removvng from the heat. Garnish with chives when serving.

TRADITIONAL CLEAR SOUP WITH PRAWNS

Serves 4

4 large prawns

4 shiitake mushrooms

4 mange tout

800ml Japanese soup stock
(see page 28)

1 tsp salt

1 tbsp sake

2 tsp soy sauce
(ideally a light coloured one)

a pinch of Umami seasoning

---

1 De-vein the prawns, parboil in salted water for 40-60 seconds, then remove the shells.

2 Remove the stems of the shiitake and trim the mange tout, then parboil them.

3 Heat up the soup stock, salt and sake, add the prawns, shiitake and soy sauce. Bring to the boil, add the Umami seasoning and remove from the heat. Garnish with the mange tout when serving.

GROUND TOFU
WITH VEGETABLES

Serves 4

200g konnyaku (1/2 size block)

100g asparagus

1/4 carrot

180g cotton tofu (1/2 size block)

2 tbsp ground sesame seeds

2 tbsp white miso

2 tbsp sugar

a pinch of Umami seasoning

1 Microwave the tofu for 2 minutes to force out excess water. Cut the konnyaku into strips, 1cm × 3cm, boil lightly. Then throw the water away and heat again to evaporate excess water.

2 Slice the asparagus diagonally, Cut the carrot into thin strips, 0.5cm × 3cm, and boil lightly.

3 Put the tofu, sesame seeds, miso, sugar and Umami seasoning in a mortar and grind with a pestle.

4 Mix the tofu mixture with the vegetables and serve.

CRISPY BURDOCK ROOT WITH SWEET AND SPICY SAUCE

Serves 4

1 large burdock root

1/4 carrot

vegetable oil

5g bonito flakes (1 small packet)

roasted sesame seeds (optional)

<A>

2 tbsp soy sauce

2 tbsp sake

1 tbsp sugar

a pinch of Umami seasoning

1   Shave cut the burdock root, soak in water for a while and drain. Cut the carrot into very thin strips.

2   Heat the oil in a frying pan and stir-fry the burdock root and carrot.

3   Add <A> to the pan and cook until the sauce is reduced to nothing. Mix in the bonito flakes and garnish with sesame seeds.

LEEK & WAKAME
WITH SWEET MISO SAUCE

Serves 4

2 leeks

100ml hot water

a pinch of Umami seasoning

5g dried wakame

<A>

2 tbsp white miso

1 tbsp sugar

1/2 tsp Japanese mustard

2 tsp rice vinegar

a pinch of Umami seasoning

1 Place the hot water, Umami seasoning and leeks in a deep pan, put a lid and cook for 3-4 minutes. Drain, leave to cool and cut into 2cm pieces.

2 Soak the wakame and cut into bite size pieces.

3 Mix <A> well then mix with leeks and wakame.

QUICK & EASY
LIGHT VEGETABLE PICKLES

Serves 4

200g cabbage

1 Japanese cucumber
(or 1/4 Western one)

1/4 carrot

2 radish

2/3 tbsp salt

a pinch of Umami seasoning

some soy sauce

---

1 Cut the vegetables into small pieces.

2 Put them in a plastic bag, add the salt and shake well. Remove the air from the bag and close with an elastic band. Leave for 20-30 minutes.

3 Squeeze the bag to force out the excess water from the vegetables, put onto a plate and sprinkle on Umami seasoning and soy sauce.

UMAMI
ON THE WORLD

Although it was only in 1985 that the word 'Umami' became international, Umami itself has been used all over the world for many years. The ingredients used vary according to the country and area, and are a reflection of its climate and food culture. This means that people have recognized the essence of Umami since ancient times. It might come as a surprise for you that so many different ingredients are used to create different types of Umami taste. Let's enjoy the Umami world trip!

*The brackets indicates the ingredient(s) of each umami.

O Umami food or seasoning made from fermented beans and/or grains. It is normally available in either paste or liquid form.

O Umami seasoning made from fermented fish, prawns and / or other seafood. Available in either paste or liquid form.

O Umami food made from other ingredients.

Europe
Anchovy Paste
(Anchovy)

Europe
Bovril
(beef extract)

Europe
Ham (por

West Africa
Dawadawa, Soumbara
(parloa bean)

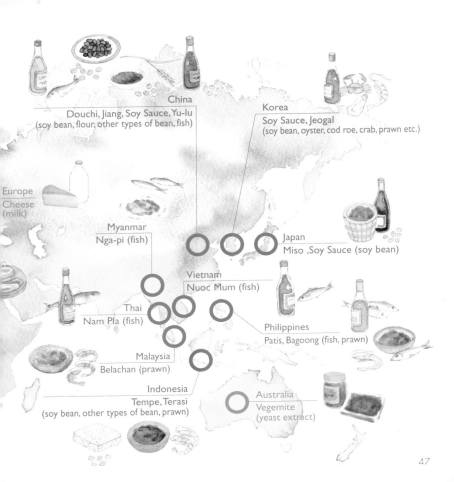

China
Douchi, Jiang, Soy Sauce, Yu-lu
(soy bean, flour, other types of bean, fish)

Korea
Soy Sauce, Jeogal
(soy bean, oyster, cod roe, crab, prawn etc.)

Europe
Cheese
(milk)

Myanmar
Nga-pi (fish)

Japan
Miso , Soy Sauce (soy bean)

Vietnam
Nuoc Mum (fish)

Thai
Nam Pla (fish)

Philippines
Patis, Bagoong (fish, prawn)

Malaysia
Belachan (prawn)

Indonesia
Tempe, Terasi
(soy bean, other types of bean, prawn)

Australia
Vegemite
(yeast extract)

The word *Umami seasoning* in this book means Monosodium Glutamate(MSG).

Approximate metric equivalents in this book
1 tbsp = 15 ml, 1/2 tbsp = 7.5ml, 1 tsp = 5ml, 1/2 tsp = 2.5ml